CROSS TOWN
·BACK BAY·COPLEY SQUARE·
·BROOKLINE·ALLSTON·
·BRIGHTON·
·WATERTOWN·NEWTON·
·SPRING HILL·
·CAMBRIDGE·ARLINGTON·

SPITTING FORBIDDEN
WITHIN THIS STATION

ALLST
P

SUB

TO
PARK ST

PUBLIC GARDEN ENT

NORTH STATION

BOYLS

PASSA
TO
SCOLLAY SC

TUNN

OUT NE

RD.

CARS
CHESTNU
CYPRE
HARVA

BENEATH THE STREETS OF BOSTON

Beneath the Streets of

BOSTON

BUILDING AMERICA'S
FIRST SUBWAY

WRITTEN & ILLUSTRATED BY

Joe McKendry

David R. Godine · Publisher

BOSTON

≋ *For Susan* ≋

ACKNOWLEDGMENTS

Many of the illustrations on this book are based upon construction photographs, drawings, and related documents in the collection of Historic New England / SPNEA. Special thanks to Lorna Condon for making them available to me. My sincere thanks, too, to Danny Cohen of the Seashore Trolley Museum for generously sharing his knowledge of Boston subway history and nineteenth-century construction methods; to Bradley Clarke of the Boston Street Railway Association for offering invaluable information and images related to Boston subway construction, history, and lore; to George Sanborn at the State Transportation Library for sharing countless stories from his encyclopedic knowledge of Boston transportation history; to Carl W. Scarbrough for his direction in shaping the book's layout and content, and to my family and friends for their generous criticism, encouragement, and support throughout the duration of this project.

First published in 2005 by
David R. Godine, Publisher
Post Office Box 450
Jaffrey, New Hampshire 03452
www.godine.com

LIBRARY OF CONGRESS CATALOGING-IN-PUBLICATION DATA
McKendry, Joe, 1972–
Beneath the streets of Boston : building America's first subway /
written & illustrated by Joe McKendry.
p.   cm.
ISBN 1-56792-284-8 (hardcover : alk. paper)
1. Subways—Massachusetts—Boston—History.
I. Title.
TF847.B7M38 2004
625.4'2'0974461—dc22
2004016418

First Edition
MANUFACTURED IN CHINA

One hundred ten years ago, downtown Boston faced traffic problems unlike any it had ever known. The area stretching from Boston Common to South Station was densely packed with businesses large and small that drew thousands of people every day. Everything from buying a hat to taking out a bank loan to visiting government offices or going to the theater brought thousands of people into the downtown business district. At its busiest, the stretch of Tremont Street running alongside Boston Common could become so crowded with trolleys and carriages that locals joked that it might be faster to climb atop the trolley cars and walk to their destinations. Knowing the situation would only deteriorate, Massachusetts Governor Frederick T. Greenhalge and Boston Mayor Nathan Matthews established the Boston Transit Commission to develop better ways to manage traffic through the city.

Boston's traffic problems surfaced during the 1890s, but their roots stretched back half a century to the years when the city's population truly began to explode. During the 1840s, Boston was the first stop in the New World for thousands of desperate and hungry immigrants fleeing Ireland's disastrous potato famine. A steady stream of immigrants from Italy, Germany, and Eastern Europe added to the numbers, and in just ten years Boston's population swelled from 90,000 to 135,000.

These newcomers often arrived with little more than the clothes on their backs. Eager to establish themselves in their adopted country, they gladly took any work that was offered, providing a steady and welcome supply of new hands for the city's manufacturers.

The widespread implementation of the steam engine as a power source for factories coincided with their arrival, enabling manufacturers to locate their businesses wherever they chose – not just near rivers, which for years had been the only source of power. Business owners, eager to take advantage of cheap labor and new technology, moved their factories to Boston and hired immigrants to operate the machinery.

Public transportation was all but non-existent. Workers had little choice but to live within walking distance of their workplaces. Unscrupulous landlords left their tenement buildings in disrepair and charged high rents – often much higher than more comfortable apartments in other parts of the city. Before long, Boston's residential areas – especially the West End and the North End – were crowded with poor families living in miserable conditions.

Boston's initial solution to the growing need for public transport was the horse-drawn trolley, which freed workers to leave the slums. Anyone could commute to work at a cost of 8 cents per day. Businessmen also made good use of the trolleys: before the invention of the telephone they had had to cross the city on foot to conduct their business. New tracks were laid at a rate that barely kept pace with demand. Residents in the nearby towns of Roxbury, Cambridge, Somerville, and South Boston came to rely on the trolley to get into the city for their everyday needs.

Before long, traffic jams had become daily nuisances, especially on Tremont Street where many of the major trolley lines converged. In 1889, electricity began replacing horse power on Boston's ever-expanding trolley system. The new source of power was cleaner and more efficient, but did little to ease the growing problem. By 1895, a crush of four hundred trolley cars joined a flood of private carriages, horse-drawn cabs, and commercial wagons during rush hour on Tremont Street – a chaotic, frustrating convergence of vehicles.

Faced with a steadily deteriorating situation, the Boston Transit Commission recommended the construction of an interconnected system of subway and elevated railway lines. The four proposed lines would connect at or near Tremont Street, the hub of the city's activity. From there, they would branch out into the surrounding communities. Boston's subway would be the first ever built in the United States; New York City had considered building a subway as early as the 1860s, but would only complete its first tunnel in 1904, seven years after Boston's first tunnel was put into service.

Public transportation systems had already met with success in Europe, but in the United States building a subway was still a new and dangerous job requiring a mastery of both terrain and technology. To understand the many challenges they were facing, engineers looked first to London, which opened an underground railroad for steam trains in 1863 and its famous 'tube' for electrically powered trains in 1890. Subways in Budapest and Glasgow, completed a year before Boston's tunnel opened, also provided engineers with useful insights.

Boston's rapid transit trains would ultimately pass under and over existing roadways. They would flow beneath Boston Harbor, span the Charles River, and tunnel through Beacon Hill. Each branch of the system would ultimately demand that the builders develop innovative construction methods.

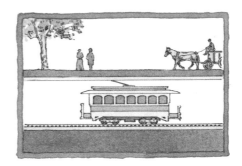

CUT-AND-COVER TUNNEL

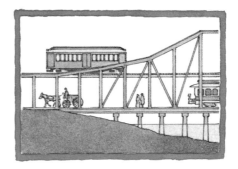

ELEVATED RAILWAY & BRIDGE

UNDERWATER TUNNEL

DEEP-BORED TUNNEL

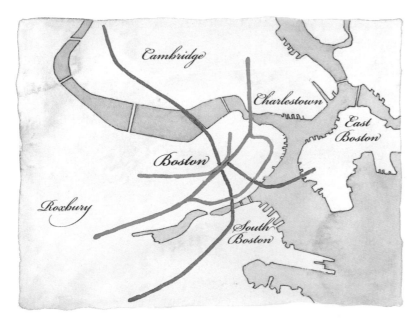

SUBWAY BILL PASSES IN CITY-WIDE VOTE 15,483–14,212.

ANTI-SUBWAY LEAGUE LOSES BATTLE.

WORRY OVER LOST BUSINESS.

BOSTON, Sept. 3—The Merchants' Anti-Subway League, started by Tremont Street business owners who are worried that the subway will take away customers by reducing street traffic, lost its battle to halt construction when the people of Boston voted 15,483 to 14,212 in favor of the subway. Yesterday's vote was brought about by the group in a petition to the Massachusetts General Court that challenged the legislative act authorizing the subway. Joining the cause were citizens opposed to tearing up the Common for purposes of subway construction, and nearby building owners, who are concerned that the subway construction will weaken the foundations of their buildings.

The lengthy fight over the form of transportation most suitable for Tremont Street has provoked heated debate. While champions of the elevated plan have praised it as cost effective, critics have described it as a "monstrosity" that would ruin the picturesque qualities of Boston Common. As a result of yesterday's vote, the "L" will not be built on Tremont Street, but plans to build a similar railway in other parts of the city have been approved.

Continued on the Second Page.

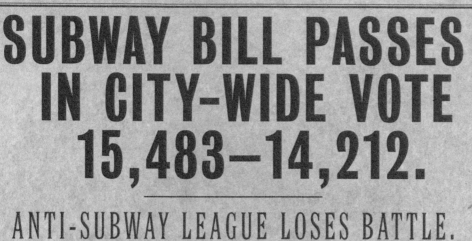

Too Many Cooks Often Spoil The Soup, and Too Many Doctors Often Spoil The Patient.

Now, here is Dr. Subway and Dr. Elevated operating on the same patient, poor old Boston, who is suffering from congestion. These doctors had a very violent quarrel as to which of their prescriptions is the better. Finally they compromise by deciding to give the patient both courses of treatment.

MANY CITIZENS REMAIN SKEPTICAL OF UNDERGROUND TRAVEL.

Fear of Evil Spirits Below Ground.

BOSTON, Sept. 3—Concerns about the healthfulness and safety of underground travel have caused many Bostonians to vow that they will never set foot in the subway. Among the concerns is the quality of the underground air, which some believe could cause serious respiratory problems. Others describe the underground realm as a place of "subterranean gloom" inhabited by evil spirits and ghosts. Still others refuse to use the subway simply because they prefer above-ground travel, traffic jams and all. I.W. Sprague, a local undertaker, said "I don't believe in a tunnel or a subway. I expect to be a long time underground after I am dead, but while I live I want to travel on earth, not under it."

Continued on the Fourth Page.

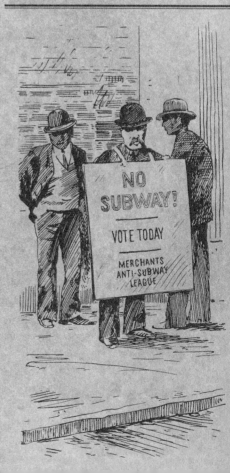

CUT-AND-COVER TUNNEL

On the morning of March 28, 1895, a groundbreaking ceremony was held on the Boston Common. Governor Greenhalge presented a shovel to Transit Commission chairman George Crocker saying, "It is my privilege to hand you this shovel, with which you are to commence the work of the subway. I hope the building of the subway will bring the relief which the people of Boston seek." After the groundbreaking, construction began.

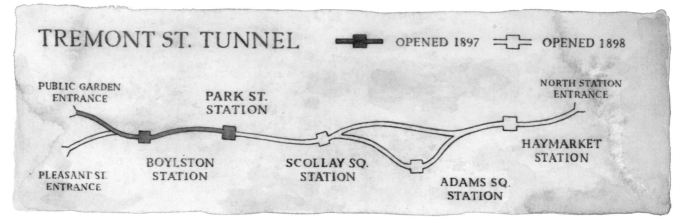

TREMONT ST. TUNNEL — OPENED 1897 — OPENED 1898

PUBLIC GARDEN
ENTRANCE

PARK ST.
STATION

NORTH STATION
ENTRANCE

HAYMARKET
STATION

PLEASANT ST.
ENTRANCE

BOYLSTON
STATION

SCOLLAY SQ.
STATION

ADAMS SQ.
STATION

Plans for the first tunnel along Tremont Street required the tangle of pipes and conduits carrying the city's utilities to be relocated and re-routed around the path of the subway. Engineers studied intricate city utility maps to determine which pipes would have to be moved. Once workers located the right pipe, service was temporarily shut down while the old utility pipes were removed and replaced with new ones.

The Tremont Street tunnel would be built and opened in two stages: the first from the Public Garden entrance to Park Street, and the second from Park Street to North Station, through stops at Scollay, Adams, and Haymarket Squares.

Subway planners laid out the route of the subway along the outer edge of the Old Common Burial ground. Only a handful of gravestones were visible along the route, so workers expected that they would have to move only a few graves to make room for the tunnel. Before they finished, they would discover the remains of more than 900 bodies in unmarked graves. The Boston Post *reported the gruesome discovery in an article headlined "Hideous Germs Lurk in the Underground Air." An illustration accompanying the article depicted a "subway microbe" enlarged 10,000 times beneath a microscope.*

THE SUBWAY MICROBE

Workers fenced off the corner of Boston Common at Park Street to start digging the tunnel. Tunnel workers, or "sandhogs," used picks and shovels to loosen the earth and load it into wooden horse carts. Some of the earth was used to level uneven ground on parts of Boston Common and Public Garden, but most was hauled away to landfills at night by gravel cars on the the Boston & Maine railroad.

To keep the earth walls of the trench from collapsing, workers built temporary wooden bracing for support. The bracing also served as a "road" for one of the most important pieces of equipment used in the subway's construction. The "traveller" was a large platform with concrete mixing equipment and wooden cranes that could be rolled across the worksite on a set of rails. Another set of rails beside the trench was used to move fresh concrete from the mixer to points along the tunnel. The same set of rails was used to carry away loads of excavated earth.

A coal-fired steam engine powered the cranes. Operators used a system of levers to control the cranes' positions and to operate the winches that paid out steel cables that raised and lowered materials into the trench.

On March 4, 1897, a disastrous explosion killed six men, two horses, and injured more than fifty people when a spark from a streetcar ignited a leaking gas pipe at the corner of Tremont and Boylston Streets. Although damage underground was minor, the blast severely damaged nearby buildings while destroying large sections of the roadway, which took several months to fully repair.

Once the trench was deep enough, work began on the walls and floor. Both were made using a combination of concrete, steel beams, reinforcing bar, and a layer of waterproof grout.

The roof of the tunnel was made by building brick arches between steel support beams, perpendicular to the tracks. Bricklayers used wooden molds to hold the shape of each arch as they placed their bricks. Once the mortar had dried, the wooden mold could be removed and re-used to create the next arch. The roof, finished with a layer of concrete and water-proofing, was then covered with soil.

Blocks of granite were shipped from a New Hampshire quarry and used to build entrances above Park Street and Boylston Street stations. Below, stairs were installed and station platforms were built.

Inside the tunnel, wooden ties were nestled into a bed of crushed-stone ballast and steel rails were fastened to them with heavy iron spikes. Overhead, electricians connected a high-voltage cable, set into a wooden track that guided the conducting rod that provided electricity to the trolley.

Residents and passersby – soon to be the subway's passengers – stopped to watch the stonemasons at work and to air their opinions about the tunnel and its new entrance buildings. Most believed the subway was a good idea, but a handful remained skeptical about traveling below ground – a place many associated with death and burial. That association colored the way some people viewed the subway: one critic described the station entrance buildings as resembling "the plainer type of mausoleums that are seen in the great cemeteries of Paris."

With most of the digging completed between the Public Garden and Park Street, work began on the details, which included replanting grass and repaving streets that construction had disrupted. To ensure a cheerful atmosphere, and to help relieve the gloom some people expected, lights were installed and a bright coat of white paint was applied to the walls and ceiling of the tunnel. Stations were furnished with benches, turnstiles, and signs to direct passengers.

Just before 6:00 A.M. on the morning of September 1, 1897, motorman James Reed and a trolley full of passengers rolled down into the tunnel. A short while later, passengers began streaming down the stairs at Boylston Street and Park Street stations.

By all accounts, the Tremont Street tunnel was an immediate success. The improvement in above-ground traffic was so dramatic and proved such a relief to commuters that one passenger described the effect being "like removing a blockade from a river."

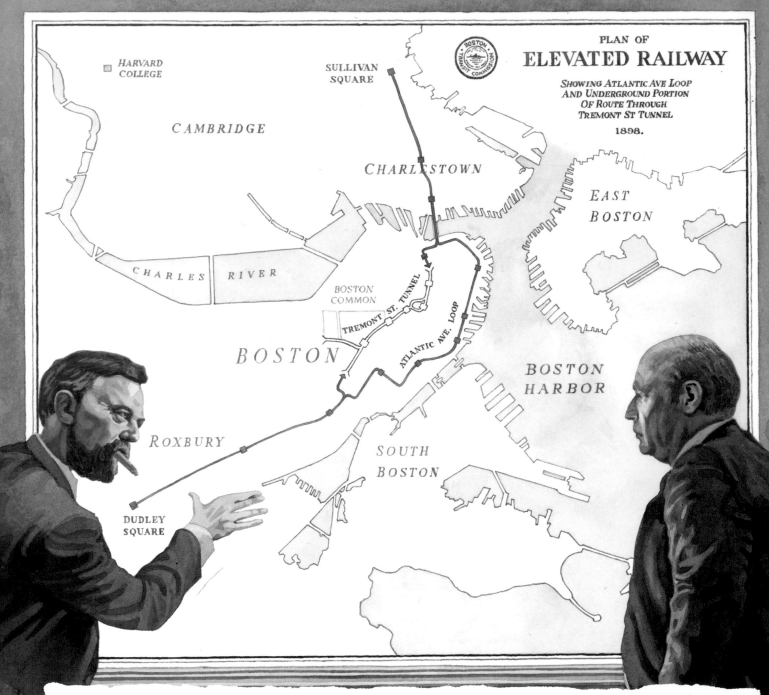

The second phase of the Tremont Street tunnel – stretching through Scollay, Adams, and Haymarket Squares to North Station – was completed in September of 1898. By this time, the Transit Commission was busy working on much more ambitious plans for an elevated railway between Sullivan Square in Charlestown and Dudley Square in Roxbury.

Building the elevated railway, or the "EL" as it became known, would be less expensive than building a tunnel, which required tearing up streets and re-routing utility lines. Plans for an elevated railway along Tremont Street had been rejected in favor of preserving the picturesque quality of the Boston Common. This time, the emphasis was more on economy than on preserving scenery. An elevated railway passing through commercial and residential areas was more acceptable than one passing beside Boston's oldest and most treasured park.

ELEVATED RAILWAY & BRIDGE

On its way to Charlestown, Boston's elevated railway would pass through Roxbury, the South End, and along the Boston waterfront, where trolleys routinely slowed to a crawl as they passed through bustling neighborhoods crowded with carriages, pushcarts, and pedestrians. The "EL" would reduce street traffic by moving commuter traffic above the roadbed. Faster, more regular service would reduce the demand for street trolleys. As the elevated tracks approached downtown Boston, they dipped below ground, sending trains through the Tremont Street tunnel on a dedicated lane. After making scheduled stops and allowing passengers to make transfers, the trains would re-emerge on the other side and climb back above street level.

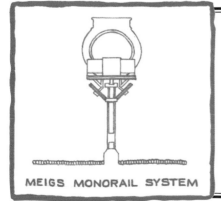

MEIGS MONORAIL SYSTEM

Officials briefly considered Joseph Meigs's monorail system (left) for Boston's "EL." The plan featured tubular, steam-powered trains riding on angled wheels. In the end the city opted for the "Manhattan system" (right) first developed in New York in the 1820s to carry steam trains through the busiest sections of town.

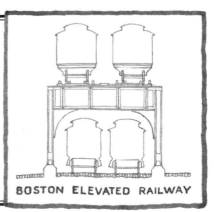

BOSTON ELEVATED RAILWAY

...ATED OF PREY
...y Waves
...affled.

...G CREWS ARE ...CHED AWAY.

...ier Likely to be ...tal Loss.

...Pounding off Hatteras.

...C, L.I., Dec. 29—The cap-
... of the steamer Drumel-
...ing been in the shadow of
... days and nights, suffer-
...ng agonies from the cold,
...this afternoon.

... was attended with the
... to the brave men who
...o accomplish it. Immedi-
... tug Catharine Moran of
...wing company, which had
...n Sandy Hook to the scene
... the two large lifeboats
...ried were launched and an
... reach the Drumelzier.

...rous surf, however, com-
...andonment of the effort
...rned to the tug. By noon,
...the imprisoned sailors
...ve that, notwithstanding
...chances sustained, anoth-
...s made.

...tossed about like a cockle-
...n and skill triumphed, and
...v were transferred to the
...ain, with the same dogged
...ch caused him to refuse
...s' assistance on Monday
...ained on board. Sixteen of
...ined with him.

...d Capt. Patterson of the
...d his tug and the rescued
...on board than more dan-
...ls were raised on the
...rough which her stubborn

ELEVATED RAILWAY UNDER CONSTRUCTION.

'L' PLAN WENT THROUGH CHANGES.

Officials Adopt a More Modest Proposal.

Elevated Trains Will Use a Modified Portion of Tremont Tunnel as They Pass Through City.

BOSTON, Dec. 31—Work began yesterday on the construction of the elevated railway system that will pass through parts of Charlestown, Boston, and Roxbury. Features will include a new bridge between Charlestown and Boston, a special reserved lane in the Tremont Street tunnel for passing through downtown and a connecting loop that will run along Atlantic Avenue, where activity surrounding the numerous wharves regularly brings street traffic to a standstill. Handsome copper stations along the route have been designed by Alexander Wadsworth Longfellow, a relative of the famous poet Henry Wadsworth Longfellow. Moving forward on its construction has come only after years of debates and alterations to a plan that has looked dramatically different in each of its stages.

Most notable among the early proposals was the 'Meigs Elevated Railway'. Joseph Meigs, its inventor, built a quarter-mile track in Cambridge to demonstrate the benefits of his tube-shaped trains and erected a sample post in Adams Square for public inspection. The public approved a bill in its favor in 1894, but Meigs' steam-powered locomotives, which billowed out thick black smoke and ran on angled wheels were later rejected in favor of the electric power and standard wheels of the 'Manhattan system', whose trains are cleaner and can be run on standard subway

---

BRYAN'S BIG DAY.

He Makes 18 Addresses in 15 Hours.

Paid Greater Attention Than Usual to the Trusts.

Traveled through Rich Farming Section.

TELLS WHY REPUBLICANS WANT A BIG ARMY.

As to "Philippine Island Lumber and Development Co."

LACROSSE, Wis. Oct. 29— When W. J. Bryan concluded his last speech here tonight, he had made 18 addresses and had covered about 15 hours of time during the day.

Beginning at 8 o'clock in the morning, he talked at intervals until 11 o'clock tonight, putting in fully six hours of speechmaking. The first speech was made at Shakopee, and after that appearance he spoke in succession at Jordan, Belle Plaine, Henderson, Lezur, St. Peter, Mankato, Janesville, Waseeka, Papciak, Dodge Center, Kasson, Rochester, St. Charles, Winona and three speeches here tonight.

The region traversed today is a rich agricultural section, and Mr. Bryan's remarks were addressed especially to farmers, the trust question receiving even a greater share of attention than usual.

At Shakopee Mr. Bryan said:

"Why is it the republican party allows the trusts to grow? Because the republican party is more interested in those who possess the organized wealth of the country than in those who are contributing to the large dividends collected by the trusts.

Continued on the Third Page.

TODAY'S GLOBE CONTENTS.

Page 1.

Board of police and nine officers guilty of neglect of duty on night of police.Tech clash, reduce five of them in

---

RHEUMATIS CURED IN A FE HOURS

Munyon's Rheumatism Cure ... pains in legs, arms, back, ... swollen joints in a few hours.

No remedy has cured so ... Rheumatism, Gout and Lumbag ... my Rheumatism Cure. Try it a ... bid goodbye to crutches, canes an ... It does not put the disease to s ... drives it from the system. Relie ... in from one to three hours, ar ... generally before one vial has be ... Munyon.

THE WEATHER

WASHING ... March 31—Fore ... Friday and Saturd ... For New Engl ... Friday and S ... warmer in the ...

Friday; light to fresh north ... winds, becoming brisk off the s ... coast.

For eastern New York, gener ... Friday and Saturday, except clo ... threatening along the coas ... northeasterly winds.

Local forecast—For Bost ... vicinity, fair weather Friday an ... bly Saturday; fresh easterly wi ...

The temperature yesterday ... cated by the thermometer at ... son's spa: 3 a m 57°, 6 a m 58°, 9 ... 12 m 65°, 3 p m 63°, 6 p m 62 ... 60°, 12 mid 60°; average tem ... yesterday 61 4-21°.

TODAY'S GLOBE CONTE

Page 5.

Winchester citizens tender r ... to Congressman S. W. McCall ... City of Chicago decided n ...

Beams for the "EL" were hoisted into place using a traveller similar to the one used to build the Tremont Street tunnel. As each section of the elevated railway was completed, the traveller was moved forward and put to work on the next section.

Once the support beams were in place, four-man "riveting gangs" began the work of assembling the framework. Working fast and with a practiced rhythm, riveting gangs raced to fasten the individual cast-iron beams, plates, and struts into a sturdy latticework. The first worker heated each rivet in a portable coal forge. Once the rivet was red hot, he used metal tongs to toss it to the second worker, who caught it in a tin bucket and placed it through pre-drilled holes in the beams. The third worker held the head of the rivet in place with a "bucking bar," while the fourth worker sealed the joint by hammering on the soft metal to form a second head.

RIVET

UNFINISHED

FINISHED

Limited space along parts of the route meant that the elevated railway would have to be built within a few feet of some second-floor apartments. Residents found their bedrooms, living rooms, and kitchens on display – forcing some to permanently close their window blinds.

LIFE WITH THE NEW ELEVATED RAILWAY

Wife to Husband: "Honey, what would you like for breakfast?"
Elevated Worker: "Bacon and Eggs would be fine, thank you!"

The seven miles of track between Charlestown and Roxbury were erected piece by piece by strong workers using little more than muscle and hand tools. Two rows of heavy wooden railroad ties were bolted to the iron framework and eighteen-yard-long sections of steel rail were nailed down on top. Alongside each set of tracks, workers installed a third rail that would provide electricity via a small metal conductor or "shoe" attached to each car.

As work continued on the streets, foundations were being prepared in the Charles River for a new bridge. The bridge would connect the elevated railway tracks between Boston and Charlestown and also provide space for street traffic, trolleys, and pedestrians.

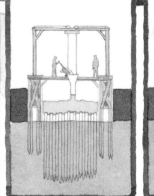
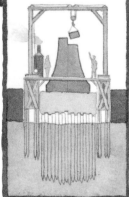

Eight rectangular side foundations and one large circular center foundation were built inside watertight enclosures called "cofferdams." First, wooden pilings were pounded into the riverbed to create a solid footing, then massive structures of granite blocks and concrete were assembled atop the footings to support the bridge.

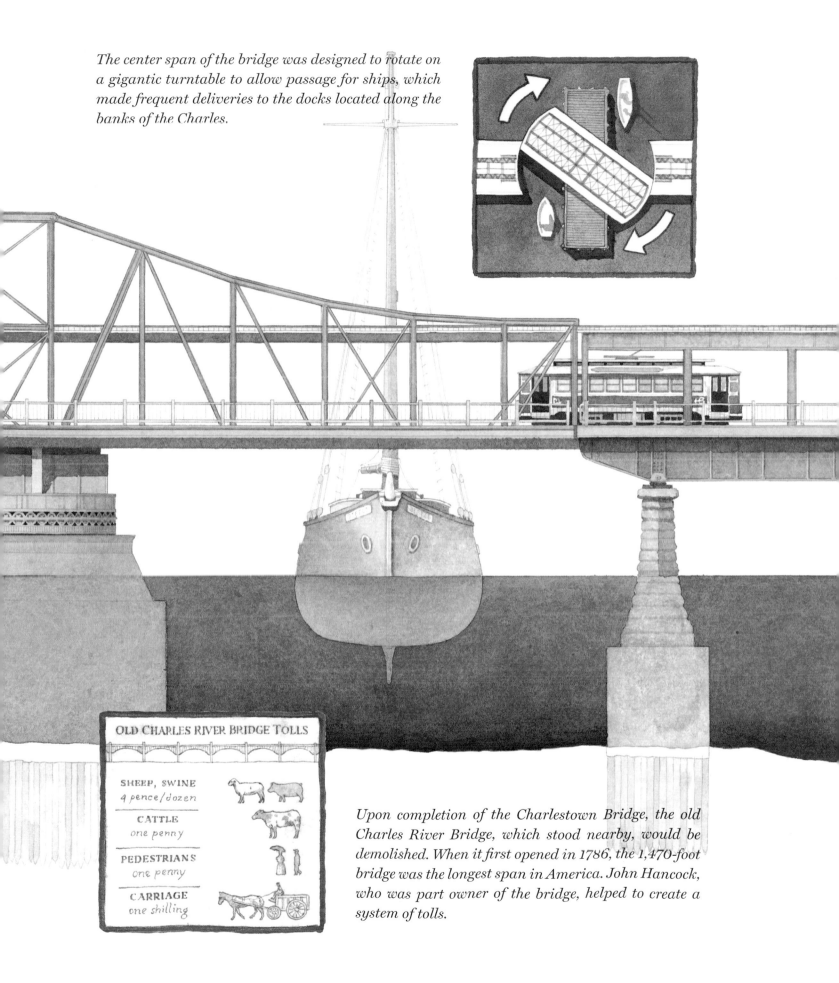

The center span of the bridge was designed to rotate on a gigantic turntable to allow passage for ships, which made frequent deliveries to the docks located along the banks of the Charles.

OLD CHARLES RIVER BRIDGE TOLLS

SHEEP, SWINE
4 pence/dozen

CATTLE
one penny

PEDESTRIANS
one penny

CARRIAGE
one shilling

Upon completion of the Charlestown Bridge, the old Charles River Bridge, which stood nearby, would be demolished. When it first opened in 1786, the 1,470-foot bridge was the longest span in America. John Hancock, who was part owner of the bridge, helped to create a system of tolls.

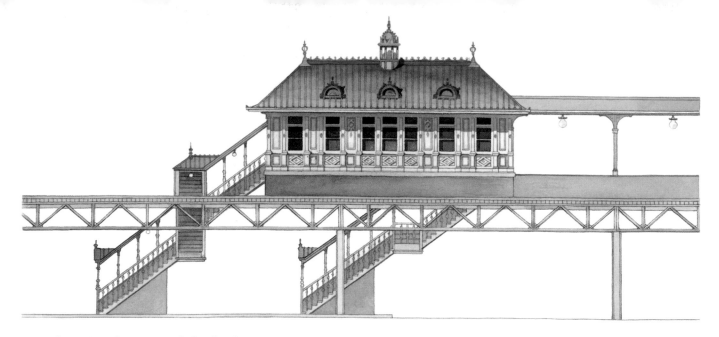

Elevation drawing of the "EL" station, after Alexander Wadsworth Longfellow Jr.'s original design.

Alexander Wadsworth Longfellow Jr. – a relative of Henry Wadsworth Longfellow, the author of *Hiawatha* – designed raised "island" stations along the route. All ten stations were built according to Longfellow's master plan, which called for elaborate architectural details in copper and wrought iron.

In the spring of 1901, finishing touches were added to the two large terminal stations at either end of the elevated railway. The ter-minals built at Sullivan and Dudley Squares were intended to serve not only the "EL" trains, but also trolleys arriving from surrounding towns. At Sullivan Square, platforms on two separate levels allowed trolleys to pull directly into the station and drop off passengers who could then transfer to the "EL." On its completion, Sullivan Square Station was the largest trolley terminal in the world.

Trains rumbled above the city's streets for the first time on June 10, 1901. Seven miles of elevated track, ten stations, and two terminals had been completed in just over 2½ years. The "EL" made stops at the train terminals, North and South Stations, the ferry terminal at Rowe's Wharf, and offered connections to the Tremont Street tunnel and dozens of trolley lines.

The successful completion of the elevated railway allowed planners to focus their attention on the third phase of the Boston Transit Commission's plan: construction of an underwater rapid transit tunnel that would create a much needed connection between Boston and East Boston. It would be the first tunnel of its kind in the United States, and once again engineers and planners faced unusual challenges as pioneers in a notoriously costly and dangerous field of construction.

UNDERWATER TUNNEL

The ferry was Boston's oldest form of mass transportation, and played a critical role in the early development of the peninsula-city. Before the industrial era, Boston's neighbors by the Charles River and Boston Harbor could easily be reached by boat. But by the early 1900s, the increasing dependence of Boston's industries on a work force housed outside city limits meant overcrowding and delays on the steam ship line connecting East Boston to the city. Impatient with slow, unreliable, and uncomfortable service, frustrated citizens demanded a better, faster, and easier way to cross the harbor.

RCH IS 50
EARS OLD.

RAL CONGREGATIONAL
ARISH OF BANGOR.

Two Pastors in Its First 47
ears of Existence.

ere the Rev Drs George
ard and George W. Field.

OR, Me, April 1— The Central
tional parish of this city,
r having had during its exis-
to three years ago only two
elebrated its semi-centennial
noon and evening. The parish
existence in 1847, largely
he endeavors of Rev Dr George
a professor for some years in
nary at Bangor, and who
the pastorship at the church
performing his duties in that

epard was one of the most
preachers of his time in New
The church was not built until
years later. Dr Shepard held
ate of the church for 16 years
$1000 per year. He resigned
ve years before his death.
rge W. Field of Boston was
ake his place. During the 30
is pastorate, Dr Field easily
he distinction of being Maine's
reacher. He served the society
few years ago, when, after
resignations, which were
naccepted, he retired from
k and now lives quietly in this

il B. Barry became the next
the church, but his stay was
t. He was succeeded by Rev
Penman of Irvington on the
.Y., who is considered a wor-
sor of Drs Shepard and Field.
h the half century the church
gaining up strength and
e.

poor little collection of people
vn to be a wealthy parish dis-
arity with a generous hand
ecting its name with every

AFTER SOME DOUBT, TUNNEL WILL BE BUILT.

Bill Ensures Rapid Transit for East Boston.

VICTORY AFTER A LONG STRUGGLE.

BATES   QUINCY

Opponents in the Battle Over the Tunnel

BOSTON, April. 1—Speaker of the
Massachusetts House of Representatives
John Bates has succeeded in passing a
bill that will requre the construction of
a rapid transit tunnel between East
Boston and Boston. Bates, a resident of
East Boston who is all too familiar with
long lines and slow trips on the ferry,
has fought for years to create a faster
way across the harbor. In 1891, Bates
worked tirelessly, often without pay on
a proposal to create a bridge to East Boston. When his efforts failed, he turned
his attention to the idea of a tunnel.

The Rapid Transit Commission's
1894 recommmendation for a city-wide
transportation system included the cre-
ation of a tunnel to East Boston. But the
legislation was worded in such a way
that allowed, but did not require it s
constuction. Mayor Quincy and other
city officials blocked the project from
going forward, refusing to put the city
in further debt with construction costs
and lost revenue from ferry tolls. Bates
continued to push for the tunnel, and
finally gained the Mayor's approval on
the condition that a 1-cent toll be
charged to passengers using the tunnel.
Many consider Bates to the 'father of

the tunnel'. One admirer suggested that
upon the death of Bates, a monument
should be erected with the inscription
"here lies Bates, who found East Boston
an island and left it a continent."

Some Still Worry About Dangers of Building an Underwater Tunnel

The proposal to build a tunnel below
Boston Harbor has made many of those
involved in the project uneasy, and not
without reason. The building of underwater tunnels is carried out by men who
must excavate thousands of cubic yards
of earth by hand in the most dangerous
of conditions. A high percentage of those
workers have suffered nerve damage or
partial paralyzation from Caisson disease as a result of working in an envi-
ronment of compressed air. Those digging at the face of the tunnel are often
victims of flooding or collapse. The only
two attempts ever made at building an
underwater rapid transit tunnel in the
United States—below the Hudson River
in New York in 1880 and below the East
River in New York in 1892—ended in
failure after separate accidents claimed
the lives of over 20 workers, causing

Work began by drilling into the soil below the harbor and bringing test samples to the surface for analysis. Planners searched for a route containing consistent, firm soil to reduce the chances of a tunnel collapse.

Once the route was determined, workers started digging the tunnel from both sides of the harbor, moving slowly toward a central meeting point. The tunnel on the East Boston side was built as a gradual slope, starting at street level so trolleys could enter the tunnel. On the Boston side, a vertical shaft was excavated to a depth of 60 feet. From that point, workers started digging in two directions; one group heading below the harbor and the other toward the Tremont Street tunnel, where the line would connect with the existing subway.

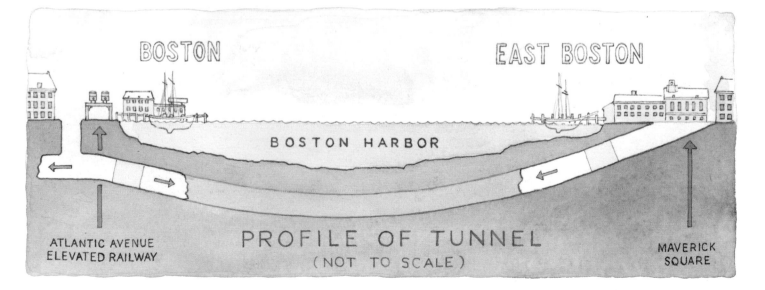

BOSTON   EAST BOSTON

BOSTON HARBOR

ATLANTIC AVENUE
ELEVATED RAILWAY

PROFILE OF TUNNEL
(NOT TO SCALE)

MAVERICK
SQUARE

Workers used a modified version of an invention called a tunnelling shield. Engineers in London had successfully built two tunnels below the Thames River using the device, whose sturdy cast-iron construction protected workers from a sudden collapse of the tunnel walls. The tunnel's arch was assembled in segments behind the rear part of the shield as sandhogs excavated beneath its forward face. As each section was finished, the shield was moved forward and the process was repeated.

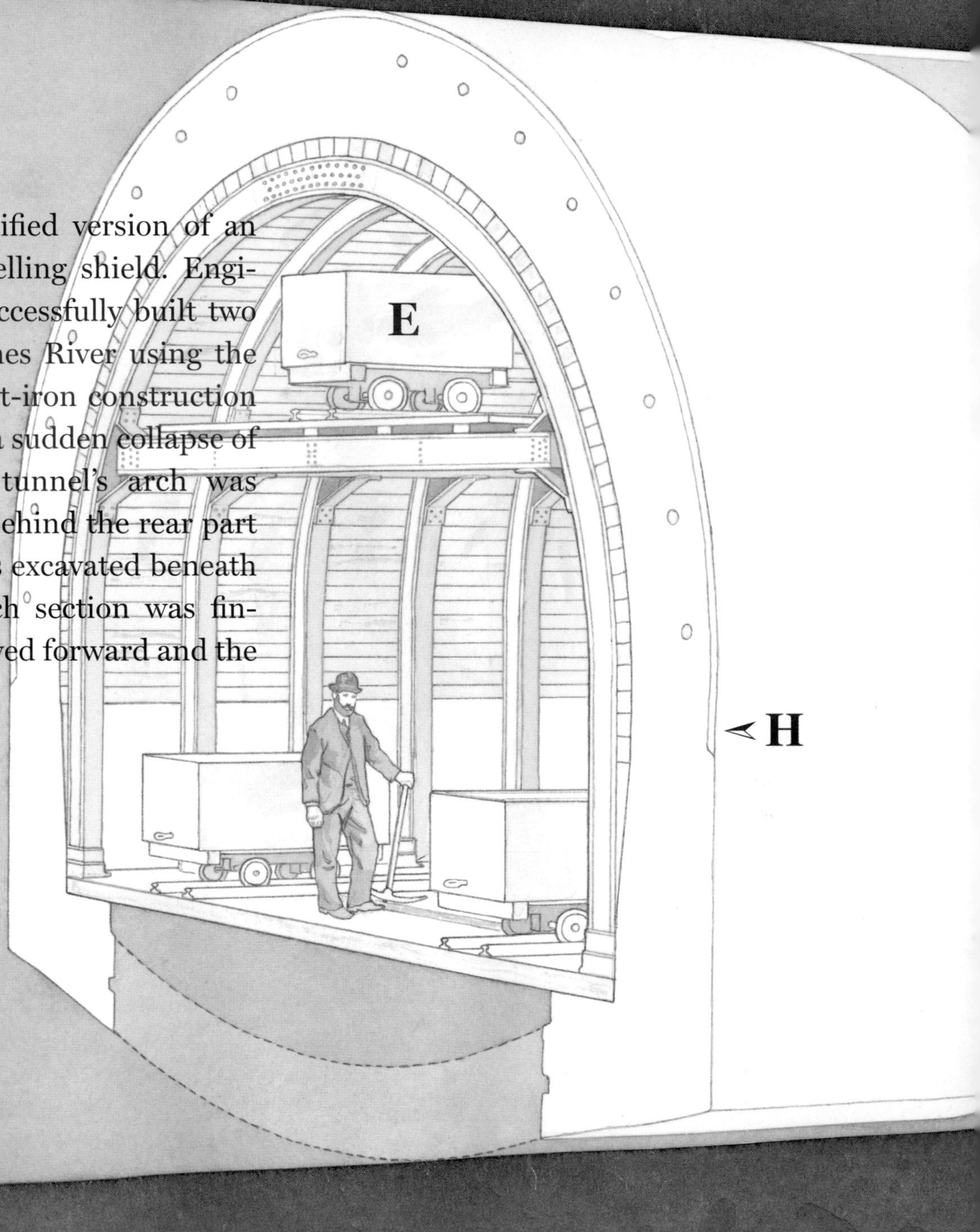

E

‹ H

A. Concrete sidewalls were built in advance to act as the "road" for the shield.

B. Workers used picks and shovels to dig beneath the face of the shield.

C. Dirt was loaded into wooden carts and rolled away on a set of tracks.

D. Steel wheels at the base of the shield allowed it to roll forward. Powerful hydraulic jacks pushed it to the next section.

E. Concrete was mixed at the tunnel entrance and delivered to the face of the tunnel in carts.

F. The concrete arch was built in sections beneath the tail of the shield.

G. A wooden mold held the shape of the arch until the concrete dried.

H. The small space left by the tail of the shield was filled with grout for water proofing.

Pressurized air was used to support the tunnel walls and prevent them from collapsing. An airlock with three chambers was installed at the tunnel entrance; one chamber served as the entry, the second an exit, and the third allowed workers to move equipment and dirt in and out of the tunnel. Workers were required to wait inside the airlocks chamber for several minutes while their bodies adjusted to the increased air pressure. Entering or leaving the tunnel too quickly could cause bubbles of nitrogen to form in the bloodstream, resulting in nerve damage, paralysis, or even death. These symptoms, known as caisson disease, or "the bends," commonly affected tunnel workers.

To make sure the two tunnel headings didn't miss each other somewhere below the harbor, workers took frequent measurements with an instrument called a transit. The transit resembled a telescope, but had tiny crosshairs on the lens that allowed workers to accurately measure the angle and distance between fixed points. By making calculations based on those findings, they were able to determine both the direction and the depth of the tunnel.

On June 19, 1903, compressed air inside the tunnel burst through a weak spot in the soil, causing part of the tunnel to collapse. The rush of escaping air knocked several workers off their feet and swept Peter Carline, who had been working near the scene of the accident, into the opening created by the blow-out. His body disappeared into the bed of the harbor, and it took workers more than a month to find his buried remains.

Conditions in the tunnel were dirty, damp, and dangerous. Using picks and shovels, workers chipped their way through earth, seashells, and stone day and night, progressing at a rate of about four feet per day. The work was carried out in two ten-hour shifts: the day shift of 120 men working from 7 A.M. to 6 P.M. and the night shift of 110 working from 7 P.M. to 6 A.M. Each shift took one one-hour break – at noon and midnight – for lunch or dinner.

East Boston tunnel to the rest of the rapid transit system. The first station on the Boston side was built directly below the Atlantic Avenue Elevated Railway. A shaft running from street level to the station floor served as a main entryway for material and workers during the tunnel's construction. After tunnelling was completed, the shaft would house elevators and one of two ventilation shafts meant to keep clean air circulating through the tunnel.

The second station was built directly under the Old State House, one of Boston's most historically significant buildings. The decision to build there was simply a matter of convenience. Its location would serve to connect the East Boston tunnel with the soon-to-be-completed Washington Street tunnel, which would serve the elevated railway trains currently using a modified portion of the Tremont St. tunnel.

A third station, at Court Street, was connected to the Tremont Street at the Scollay Square station.

As the two tunnel headings progressed toward a central meeting point below the harbor, work was underway beneath the streets on three stations that would link the

The Old State House was built in 1713 as a meeting house for the British Governor. In 1770, the Boston Massacre took place a few feet from the building, and on July 18, 1776 the Declaration of Independence was read publicly to Bostonians for the first time from its ornate balcony.

Work was carried out very carefully under the watchful eye of Boston's historical societies, which insisted that the building's appearance be altered as little as possible. Although the above-ground portion of the Old State House changed very little, the basement was demolished to make room for the new station.

On July 4, 1903 the two sides of the tunnel met below Boston Harbor, completing the underwater route between East Boston and Boston. In the following months, tracks, electric wires, and ventilation pipes were installed, and on December 30, 1904 the tunnel opened to traffic.

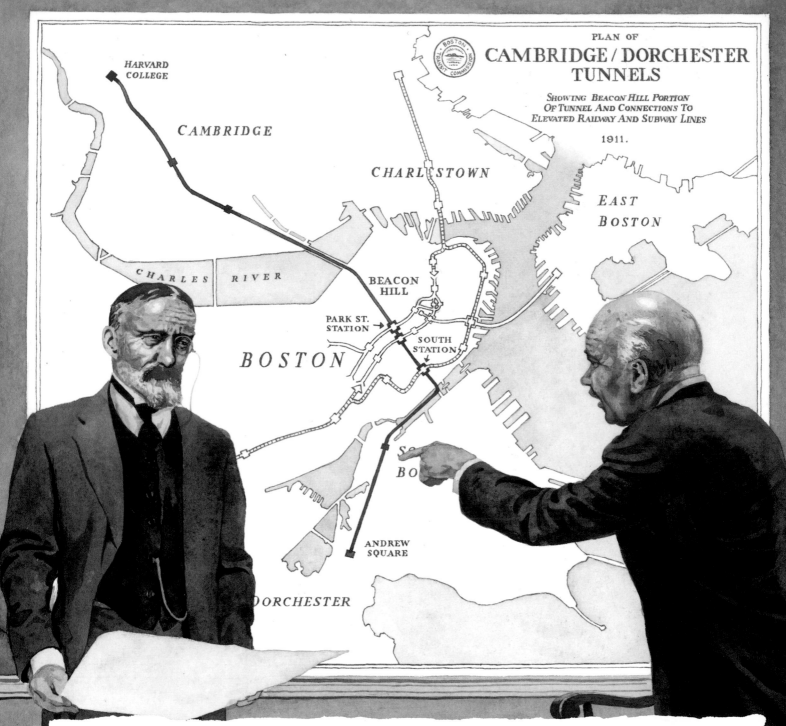

The East Boston Tunnel drastically reduced the time it took to cross the harbor. A trip that had often taken more than twenty minutes by ferry now lasted only seven minutes. At the tunnel's opening, John Bates, who had sponsored the bill ensuring the tunnel's construction and who had subsequently been elected Governor of Massachusetts, was hailed as "the man who found East Boston an island and left it a continent."

The fourth phase of construction would be a two-part project. The Cambridge tunnel – running from Harvard Square in Cambridge through Park Street Station – and the Dorchester tunnel – from Park Street to Andrew Square in South Boston near the Dorchester line – would together constitute the longest tunnel in Boston's rapid transit system.

DEEP-BORED TUNNEL

As early as 1850, Cambridge, South Boston, and Dorchester were sizeable communities with expanding populations and a growing appetite for efficient transportation. The large student population at Harvard University and other colleges in Cambridge created an increasing demand for a fast connection to the city.

The rapid growth of South Boston and Dorchester as centers of manufacturing and industry further strained a trolley system that was already struggling to serve a population that had nearly doubled in just fifteen years. During summer months, trolleys became especially overcrowded as large numbers of people from all over the city flocked to South Boston's Marine Park to enjoy the cool ocean breezes along the boardwalk.

PEAKS MANY TONGUES.

E. FLEISCHNER KNOWS TEN LANGUAGES.

e Sam Makes Use of His Talents in the Boston Postoffice.

When a foreigner gets tan-
d up in linguistic difficul-
 at the Boston Postoffice,
cle Sam immediately
ds for Herbert E. Fleisch-
, who has 10 different lan-
ages, both ancient and
dern, at his command.

hese include French,
rman, Italian, Spanish,
tuguese, Dutch, Russian,
edish, Dano-Norwegian
 Greek.

Before being employed in
 postoffice he served the
ernment at Washington,
t as translator in the mil-
ry information division
ce of the chief of staff in
 war department and in a
ilar capacity in the depart-
t of naval intelligence.

He has had naval and mil-
y translations published
he Army and Naval jour-
, and in the Army and
vy Register.

ust now he is translating
echnical book from the
man.

orn in Boston.

Mr. Fleischner was born in
ton 27 years ago, and is
 of several children of
o and Addie Hosmer
ischner.

He attended the Highland
 William H. Hodgkins
ools in Somerville and
 graduated from the
merville Latin School in
3.

He was determined to
k his way through col-
, and in order to do this
went to work in a piano
ory the day after he fin-
d his studies at the high

SIGNIFICANT PROGRESS ALREADY MADE ON CAMBRIDGE TUNNEL.

New Subway Tunnel Will Run From Harvard Square, Cambridge to Andrew Square, South Boston.

CAMBRIDGE, Jan. 8—
The Boston Transit Commission has announced that the
tunnel currently under construction between Harvard
Square and Park Street will
be extended into South Boston as far as Andrew Square,
near the Dorchester line. The
extension, referred to by subway officals as the Dorchester Tunnel, will have stations
at Washington Street and
Dewey Square in Boston, and
at Broadway and Andrew
Square in South Boston. The
tunnel will no doubt be
appreciated by the citizens of
South Boston and Dorchester,
who at present have no direct
access to rapid transit. The
stations at Broadway and
Andrew Square will serve as
major transfer points for surface trolleys, whose routes
and schedules will be drastically affected once the tunnel
is built. The stations at Washington Street and Dewey
Square will allow for conven-
ient transfers to the Washington Street tunnel, the
Atlantic Avenue 'El' and the
South Station train terminal.

Construction of the Cam-
bridge tunnel has progressed
rapidly since it began on May
24, 1909. Significant portions
of the tunnel have already
been completed along Massachusetts Avenue, which is
being torn up and recon-
structed as the tunnel is
being built. Stations along
the route will be located at
Harvard, Central, and Ken-
dall Squares. Meanwhile, the
Beacon Hill portion of the
tunnel has been excavated to
a point roughly half-way
through the hill. Progress has
been hindered somewhat by
the recent discovery of several long-forgotten wells, esti-
mated to be about 100 years
old, which were once used to
furnish water to residents.

DR CASTLE HAS BRED FOUR NEW ANIM

They Are the Cinnamon Guinea Pig, the Silver Gu and Two Distinct Species of Rats—Harvard F Lectures On His Wonderful Work at the Lowell —Value of His Experiments Should Be of Econom in the Production of Food Animals.

A great deal of interest
and literature are based upon
the fact that Luther Burbank
has made some remarkable
experiments with plants and
has produced some forms
that are new to science.

Most persons who read of
these things have the idea
that Burbank is the only per-
son in the world doing this
kind of work and do not real-
ize that perhaps the most
remarkable experiments of
the kind have been done in
Boston by Dr William Ernest
Castle, who has been experi-
menting with rats, mice, and
guinea pigs in a laboratory
belonging to Harvard Uni-
versity in one of the parks of
the metropolis.

These experiments do not
in the least detract from the
ingeniousness of Burbank,
who is the successful repre-
sentative of a hundred botan-
ists, who for nearly 50 years
have been at work crossing
plants and flowers. Such an
experimenter is Dr Ezra
Brainerd, formerly president
of Middlebury College, whose
chosen flower is the violet, of
which he has succeeded in
producing many strange and
interesting varieties.

In the matter of animals,
Dr Castle has just set forth
his results in a series of lec-
tures before the Lowell Insti-
tute, in which some of the
announcements of animals
new to science were made to
the audience even in advance
of their presentation through
the columns of the scientific
magazines.

What Dr Castle has been

pig, the cinnamon
were not known to
ists until his were ey
ver guinea pig also
science, and two kind
that are far enough
color to be called vari
though they were rea
the same original an

The manufactu
these four new ani
really glory enough
man, but they form
portion of Dr Castl
with his assistants ir
mulating of the pr
whereby the chang
been worked.

Value is Economic.

In the first place i
be understood tha
experiments as these
merely scientific
ments, but they h
highest probable e
importance. It is this
evolution that has p
on the pinnacle that
gained, and upon it
depend to maintain
there.

His future must
itself to what he can
the earth, for no mat
proudly the cities m
up their heads it is tr
food supplies must
them from the count
must ever be depende
agriculture. The kno
then, of how to prod
best animals and pla
be of the greatest
tance.

The art of breedi
course, very old. The
people were agricultu
they developed good

At the Charles River, workers built an incline to connect the tunnel with the newly completed Longfellow Bridge. The center lane of the bridge was designed to accommodate tracks for subway cars passing back and forth between Cambridge and Boston.

On the Boston side of the Longfellow Bridge, workers cut into the flank of Beacon Hill. The steep, narrow streets forced planners to abandon the cut-and-cover method used in Cambridge. Instead, they burrowed deep below one of Boston's oldest and most densely populated neighborhoods.

To Cambridge

Due to the density of homes in the neighborhood, the tunnel entrance had to cut directly through the lower floors and basements of some buildings. Residents living on those floors were forced to relocate temporarily to make room for the subway.

Work was again carried out beneath an iron tunnelling shield like the one used in the East Boston Tunnel. But this time, the firmer soil meant the shield could be used without compressed air and airlocks. As they dug, workers came across long-abandoned wells and other traces of the city's past.

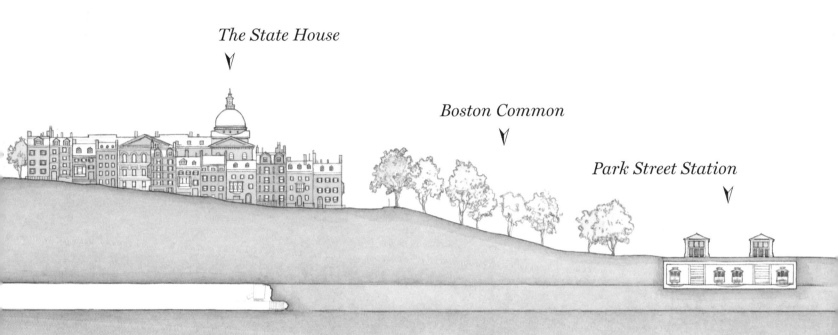

The State House

Boston Common

Park Street Station

On the other side of Beacon Hill, the tunnel continued beneath the Boston Common to a point directly below Park Street station, where work began on "Park Street Under." The new station would include a set of staircases that allowed passengers to transfer between the Cambridge/Dorchester line and the Tremont Street tunnel. Steel beams supported the upper station so work could be carried out without disrupting traffic above.

Beyond Park Street, the tunnel was extended toward today's "Downtown Crossing," the busiest shopping district in the city. The intersection of Winter, Summer, and Washington Streets was flanked by Boston's largest department stores, Jordan Marsh and Filene's. The underground construction was covered with heavy wooden planks so shoppers, carriages, and trolleys could go about their business above ground undisturbed.

Jordan Marsh Department Store was founded in 1841 by Eban Jordan, an innovative and generous businessman whose contributions to Boston included the Boston Globe, Jordan Hall, and the Majestic Theatre. Eban Jordan was also responsible for bringing the elevated railway and subway under one management. At a crucial moment in 1897, a group of investors led by Jordan acquired the West End Street Railway Company, which owned and operated the subway. Under the supervision of the Boston Transit Commission, they then leased the subway to the Boston Elevated Railway Company, a compromise that staved off the difficulties of competing transit companies and laid the groundwork for an efficient, interconnected system.

EBAN JORDAN

At Dewey Square, a subway station was built just yards from the Atlantic Avenue elevated railway and the South Station train terminal, the final stop for trains arriving from points west and south of the city, including New York, Philadelphia, and Washington D.C. Once the subway began running trains through the new tunnel, local commuters transferring from the "EL" and out-of-towners arriving at South Station would make the Dewey Square station one of the busiest in the Boston system.

After building a short tunnel below the Fort Point Channel, work began on the final stretch of construction: a cut-and-cover tunnel and stations at Broadway and at Andrew Square. The entire length of Dorchester Avenue between the two stations was torn up by work crews, forcing carriages and trolleys onto side streets.

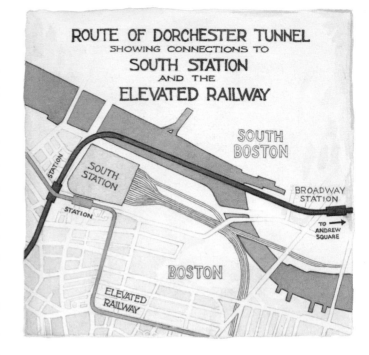

By the spring of 1918, Broadway station was finished and work on the Andrew Square terminal was well underway. Within a few months the entire tunnel from Harvard Square to Andrew Square would be complete.

On July 1, 1918, the tunnel opened to the public, and for the first time, subway trains carried passengers between Cambridge and South Boston. This important piece of the Boston Transit Commission's master plan completed a rapid transit system that reached out in all directions and made travel in Boston and its surrounding communities faster, cheaper, and more dependable than ever before.

Boston's subway introduced America to a new form of urban transportation, and soon other cities followed with subways of their own. Innovative engineering and construction set precedents in the field of subway construction and served as models for builders in years to come.

From the very beginning, Boston's rapid transit system has been a work in progress. Under the management of the Massachusetts Bay Transit Authority, the "T," as it is now called, continues to make changes, improvements, and expansions in response to the changing needs of its riders.

The four rapid transit lines built around the turn of the twentieth century have since been modernized, each line now identified by a color representing the area it serves: the Green line passes through Frederick Law Olmsted's "Emerald Necklace" park system; the Orange line passes beneath Washington Street, long ago called Orange Street; the Blue line passes beneath the waters of Boston Harbor; and the Red line honors Harvard University's official color, crimson. Even after decades of improvements, the subway's original builders would still recognize much of their handiwork. Although the last section of elevated railway was demolished in 1987, over 95% of the original subway tunnels remain in use today.

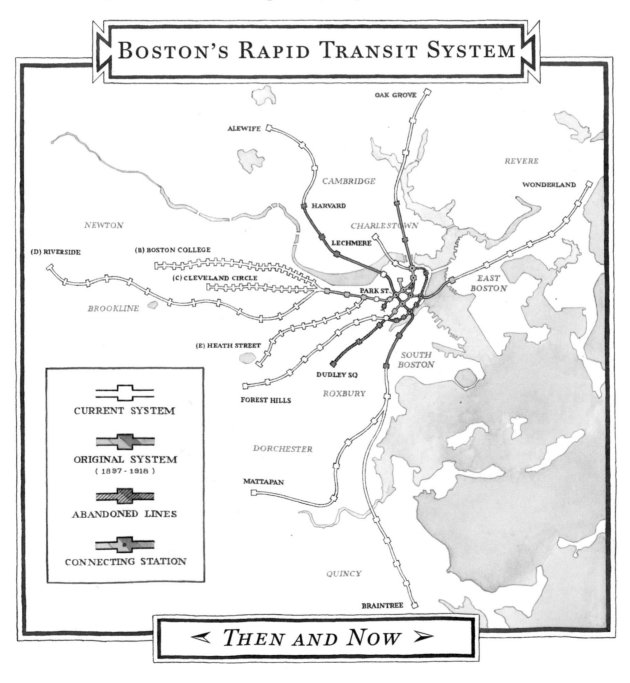

BOSTON'S RAPID TRANSIT SYSTEM

OAK GROVE

ALEWIFE

REVERE

CAMBRIDGE

WONDERLAND

HARVARD

NEWTON

CHARLESTOWN

LECHMERE

(D) RIVERSIDE   (B) BOSTON COLLEGE

(C) CLEVELAND CIRCLE

EAST BOSTON

PARK ST.

BROOKLINE

(E) HEATH STREET

SOUTH BOSTON

DUDLEY SQ

ROXBURY

FOREST HILLS

CURRENT SYSTEM

ORIGINAL SYSTEM
(1897 - 1918)

DORCHESTER

ABANDONED LINES

MATTAPAN

CONNECTING STATION

QUINCY

BRAINTREE

≺ THEN AND NOW ≻